MATHEMATICS CURRICULUM
Maths Word Problems

Year 3

Lizzie Marsland

Acknowledgements:

Author: Lizzie Marsland

Series Editor: Peter Sumner

Cover and Page Design: Kathryn Webster

The right of Lizzie Marsland to be identified as the author of this publication has been asserted by her in accordance with the Copyright, Designs and Patents Act 1998.

HeadStart Primary Ltd
Elker Lane
Clitheroe
BB7 9HZ

T. 01200 423405
E. info@headstartprimary.com
www.headstartprimary.com

Published by HeadStart Primary Ltd 2015 © **HeadStart Primary Ltd 2015**

A record for this book is available from the British Library -
ISBN: 978-1-908767-28-8

INTRODUCTION

Year 3: NUMBER - Number and place value

Year 3: NUMBER- Addition and subtraction

Year 3: NUMBER - Multiplication and division

Year 3: NUMBER - Fractions

hello

Year 3: MEASUREMENT

CONTENTS

Year 3: GEOMETRY - Properties of shapes

Year 3: STATISTICS

INTRODUCTION

These problems have been written in line with the objectives from the Mathematics Curriculum. Questions have been written to match all appropriate objectives from each 'content domain' of the curriculum.

Solving problems and mathematical reasoning in context is one of the most difficult skills for children to master; a 'real life', written problem is an abstract concept and children need opportunities to practise and consolidate their problem-solving techniques.

As each content domain is taught, the skills learnt can be applied to the relevant problems. This means that a particular objective can be reinforced and problem-solving and reasoning skills further developed. The pages can be reproduced and used either within or outside the mathematics lesson at school. They are also very useful as a homework resource.

The questions are arranged, in general, so that the more difficult questions come towards the bottom of the page. This means that differentiation can be achieved with the lower ability children working through the earlier questions and the higher ability going on to complete the whole page. The CD-ROM contains editable copies of each page. These can be edited and saved, as required, to provide extra practice or additional differentiated problems. The electronic versions on the CD-ROM can also be used on an interactive whiteboard, facilitating class discussion and investigation.

An example of a step-by-step method to solve word problems can be found on the following page. This can be edited, enlarged or used as a poster for classroom display and/or copies given to each child to be used as a check for each question answered.

Important parts of each question have been highlighted in 'bold' font. Once children have become more proficient at problem solving, it may be appropriate to remove these prompts on the editable page. Children can then be encouraged to use a highlighter or underline the important parts themselves.

Since a structured approach to problem solving supports learning, developing a whole-school approach is very worthwhile.

TO SOLVE A WORD PROBLEM

Follow these steps:

1 Read the problem carefully.

2 Find the question.

3 Identify the important parts.

4 Decide on the operation or operations.

5 Carry out the operation or operations.

6 Check your answer.

7 Feel very pleased with yourself.

NUMBER

Number and place value

These are all about number and place value!

Count from 0 in multiples of 4, 8, 50 and 100

1 James is counting in multiples of **4**. The **first** number he says is **0**. What is the **third** number he says? 8

2 Ayesha is making an apple pie. She already has **4** apples and then buys **4** more. Her grandma also gives her **4** apples. How many apples does she have altogether? 12

3 Ella counts **eight** birds in the sky. She then sees **8** more. How many birds has she counted altogether? 16

4 Mrs Brown asked her class to count in multiples of **8**. The **first** number they said was **8**. What was the **fourth** number they said? 32

5 Mollie and Paul are counting in multiples of **50**. They start counting at **0**. What are the next **two** numbers they count? 50 & 100

6 Aimee and Angus counted the cows in **3** fields. Each field had **100** cows eating grass. How many cows were there altogether? 300

Name ....

Count from 0 in multiples of 4, 8, 50 and 100

1 Bella is counting in multiples of **four**. The **first** number she says is **4**. What is the **third** number she says? *12*

2 Olivia has **8** colouring pencils. Jessica has **sixteen**. How many more colouring pencils does Jessica have? *8*

3 Omar and Marley like to count in **hundreds** together. If the **first** number they said was **0**, what was the **fourth** number they said? *400*

4 Kate is counting in multiples of **50**. She starts at **0**.
Write the next **three** numbers that she counts. *50 100 150*

5 Finn and **four** of his friends are taking turns to count up in steps of **100**.
If Finn starts counting at **0**, what number would they count up to? *400*

6 Mrs Taylor writes this number pattern on the whiteboard. Can you fill in the missing numbers?

| 0 | 4 | 8 | *12* | 16 | *20* | *24* |

Count in and use multiples of 2, 3, 4, 5, 50 and 100

1 Yousef is counting in multiples of **two**. His **first** number is **2**. What would be the next number he counts?   4

2 How many multiples of **four** should Poppy be able to find that are less than **19**?   4

3 Becky has **4** cakes. Jakub has **4** cakes and Cara has **4** cakes. How many cakes do they have altogether?   12

4 Mrs Whelan asks her class how many multiples of **five** they can count between **50** and **100**. What did they tell her?   55 60 65 70 75 80 85 90 95
9.

5 Jodi is counting in multiples of **100**. Her **first three** numbers are **566, 666** and **766**. What would the next number in her sequence be?   866

6 Ben thinks of a number and multiplies it by **3**. His answer is **15**. What was the number Ben thought of?   5

Count in and use multiples of 2, 3, 4, 5, 50 and 100

1 Jack counts in multiples of **three**. He starts at number **6**. What number does he count next? 9

2 Year 3 are counting in multiples of **two**. They start at number **10**. What are the next **three** numbers they say? 12 16 18

3 Sian has **25** teddy bears. She gets **5** more teddy bears for her birthday. How many teddy bears does she have now? 30

4 Declan is counting up in **fours**. He starts at number **16**. Which **two** numbers does he say next? 20 24

5 Sol starts at the number **40** and he counts up **three** more **fifties**. Which number does he stop at? 190

6 Miss Price asks her class to count in multiples of **100**, starting from **132**. Which **four** numbers should they say next? 232 332 432 532

4

Name ....

Find 10 or 100 more or less than a given number

1 If Ben has **200** raisins and eats **100** of the raisins at lunchtime, how many does he have left for home time?   100 ✓

2 Raqeeb has **87** marbles. He gives **10** to his friend, Jake. How many marbles does Raqeeb have left?   77 ✓

3 Celia counts forward **ten**. She starts at **64**. What number does she count up to?   74 ✓

4 There are **25** candles on the birthday cake. Josh blows out **10** of the candles. How many burning candles are left?   15 ✓

5 Luca has collected **224** football cards. For his birthday, his dad buys him another **100** cards. How many does he have now?   324 ✓

6 Nassima is **seven** years old. Her brother, Adnan, is **10** years older than her. How old is Adnan?   17   older ✓

Find 10 or 100 more or less than a given number

1   Ania has baked **58** cupcakes. Her friends eat **10**. How many cupcakes are left?

48 ✓

2   Mr Peabody asks his class to count **100** less than **347**. What number should the class say?

247 ✓

3   Abdul counts **86** sheep in Field **A**. **10** sheep are moved to Field **B** by Farmer Jim. How many sheep are left in Field **A**?

76 ✓

4   There are **72** children on the playground. **10** more children go out to play. How many children are on the playground now?

82 ✓

5   Samantha starts at **334** and then counts forward **one hundred**. What number does she count to?

434 ✓

6   Alice has saved **£256** pounds in her piggy bank. She spends **£100** on new clothes. How much money does she have left?

£156 ✓

Recognise the place value of each digit in a three-digit number (hundreds, tens and ones)

1 There are **252** pupils at Apple Tree Primary School. How many **hundreds** are there? *2.*

2 Katie counts **335** flowers in the park. She then partitions the number of flowers into **hundreds, tens** and **ones**. How many **tens** are there? *60*

3 Charlie partitions the number **528** into **hundreds, tens** and **ones**. How many **hundreds** are there? *5*

4 Miss Bell asks her class to partition **764** into **hundreds, tens** and **ones**. How many **ones** are there?

5 Katie has to write down the value of the digit **6** in the number **463**. What should she write?

6 Alfie has partitioned a number into **hundreds, tens** and **ones** and it looks like this:

300 + 20 + 9

What was the number?

Recognise the place value of each digit in a three-digit number (hundreds, tens and ones)

1 Lola partitions **482** into **hundreds**, **tens** and **ones**. How would she write this down?

2 Rafiq partitioned the number below. What number did he start with?

200 + 80 + 7

3 Rafiq partitions another number in a different way. What was the number?

700 + 30 + 16

4 Rachel's dad has forgotten about place value. He tells Rachel that the digit **4** in the number **649** is worth **400**. Is he correct? Explain your answer.

5 Mohammed says, "The value of the digit **5** in the number **562** is **50**." Is he correct? Explain your answer.

8

Name ....

Compare and order numbers up to 1000

1 Nadia had to find out which number was smaller: **482** or **428**. Which one did she choose? How did she know?

2 Jessica put the following numbers in order from largest to smallest. What does her new list look like?

310	305	300	320

3 Tom's teacher asks him to write a **three-digit** number that is larger than **535**, but smaller than **537**. What number should he write?

4 Naheed had to find out which was smaller: **224** or **242**. Which one did he choose? How did he know?

5 Write down a number that is smaller than **350**, but larger than **348**.

6 Miss Collins asks her class to put the following numbers in order of size, starting with the smallest. Can you help?

345	435	354	543	534

Name ....

Compare and order numbers up to 1000

1 Here is a sequence of numbers. Put the numbers in order of size from smallest to largest.

882   820   865   840

2 Celina is trying to decide which number is larger: **895** or **859**. Which one should she choose?

3 Jack puts these numbers in order of size from largest to smallest. What do you think his new list looks like?

658   641   690   630

4 Mr Watson asked his class to write down a number which was larger than **489** but smaller than **491**. What number should they choose?

5 Zara wants to put these numbers in order of size from largest to smallest. What would her new list of numbers look like?

981   918   891   819   899

Identify, represent and estimate numbers using different representations

1 Bertie counts **26** bees making honey. Is this number of bees nearer to **20** or **30**?

2 Oscar jumps **6 metres** in the long jump. Holly jumps **7 metres**. Who jumped further?

3 Sam throws a ball **13 metres** for his dog, Bruno. Is this nearer to **10 metres** or **20 metres**?

4 There are **70** children singing in the school choir. **36** are girls and **34** are boys. Are there more girls or boys singing in the choir?

5 Mr Rajan asks Adam what number comes exactly halfway between **40** and **60**. What number should Adam say?

6 Anastasia is **115 cm** tall. Her friend, Riley, is **10 cm** taller than her. Benny is **135 cm** tall. Who is the tallest?

Name ....

Identify, represent and estimate numbers using different representations

1 Mrs Smith gave **145 millilitres** of milk to her cat, Tiddles. Was this amount nearer to **100** or **200 millilitres**? *100* ✓

2 Daniel says, "The number which comes exactly halfway between **60** and **80** is **70**." Is Daniel correct? Explain your answer. *yes* ✓

3 There are **796** fans cheering on Redton United. Is the number of fans nearer to **790** or **800**? Explain your answer. *800* ✓

4 **26** boys and **24** girls went to the school party. How many boxes of blackcurrant juice cartons should Mr Foster buy to give the children a drink each, if blackcurrant juice cartons come in boxes of **10**? *5* ✓

5 Casper has a bottle containing **786 millilitres** of orange juice. He drinks **100 millilitres**. How much orange juice does he have left in the bottle, to the nearest **100 ml**? *700* ✓

Read and write numbers up to 1000 in numerals and words

1 Mr Baker asks his class to write the number **72** in words. How would the class write this number?

2 Poppy's teacher asks her to write the number **two hundred and thirty** in numerals. What should Poppy write?

3 Alishba lives at number **three hundred and forty three**. Her dad is making a sign for their home. Which numerals should he write on the sign?

4 Jack writes the number **eight hundred and sixty two** in numerals. Which numerals does he write?

5 Abraham writes the number **787** in words. What does he write?

6 Jade's mum asks her to write the number **853** in words. What should she write?

Name ....

Read and write numbers up to 1000 in numerals and words

1 Bilal is writing a birthday card for his friend, Charles. Charles is going to be **8**. How would he write this number in the card using a word?

2 Laura counts **fifteen** birds in the sky. How would she write this as a numeral?

3 Mr Iqbal asked Clara to write the number **252** on the whiteboard in words. What should she write?

4 Brandon reads the number **four hundred and sixty four**. How would he write this using numerals?

5 Dom writes the number **348** in words. Which words does he write?

6 Leanne's little sister has forgotten how to write the number **876** in words. What are the words that she should write?

Name ....

Solve problems involving number and place value (money)

1 How much change does Ryan get from **£1**, if he buys a lollipop for **10p**?

2 Charlotte has **267 pence** in her money jar. Write this as an amount of pounds.

3 Mum has **£300**. She gives **£100** to each of her daughters, Kate and Rose. How much money does Mum have left?

4 Which amount of money is bigger: **£389** or **£398**?

5 If you could choose, would you rather have the value of the **5** in **£650** or the value of the **5** in **£975**?

6 Mrs Jenkins sees that a washing machine is on offer for **one hundred and twenty six pounds**. How would you write this using numbers and the pound sign?

15

Name ....

Solve problems involving number and place value (distance and capacity)

1 A bottle holds **100 millilitres** of water. How much water is left if Connor drinks **10 millilitres**?

2 Mina swam **6** lengths on Monday, **2** more than this on Wednesday and **7** lengths on Thursday. On which day did she swim the most lengths?

3 Kira has a piece of string which is **123 cm** long. Billy has a piece of string which is **132 cm** long. Who has the longer piece of string?

4 Eli is going on holiday. His suitcase weighs **14 kg**. Is the weight of his suitcase nearer to **10 kg** or **20 kg**?

5 Tom's dad drives **267** miles to Blackpool. On the way back, he goes a different way and drives **276** miles. Which route was quicker? Explain your answer.

Solve mixed problems involving number and place value

1 There are **120** crisps in a big bag. Pablo shares them with his friends and they eat **100** crisps altogether. How many crisps are left?

2 **26** children go on a camping trip. Is the number of children on the trip nearer to **20** or **30**?

3 There are **36** bouncy balls in one tub and **10** in another tub. How many are there altogether?

4 Marek wrote down a number that is more than **200** and a multiple of **four**. It is less than **205**. What number did he write?

5 Liam is **18** and Jasmin is **12** years younger than Liam. Their cousin Edward is **14**. Who is the eldest and who is the youngest?

6 Shana has a good way of checking whether a whole number is multiple of **5**. What do you think her method is?

Name ....

Solve mixed problems involving number and place value

1 Jamie is counting forward in **tens**. He starts at **92** and then counts on **2** more **tens**. What number does he count up to?

2 Write the number **256** in words.

3 Hamish puts **500 grams** of soil in his plant pot. Then he adds another **4** scoops of soil, each containing **100 grams**. How many **grams** of soil are in the plant pot now?

4 Shannon has partitioned a number into **hundreds**, **tens** and **ones** and it looks like this: **600 + 40 + 3**.

What was the number?

5 Natalie has written **36** party invitations. She hands **10** invitations out to her friends at school and **10** to her friends at Brownies. How many invitations does she have left to give out?

Solve mixed problems involving number and place value

1 Natasha counts **46** cows in a field. Is the number of cows nearer to **40** or **50**?

2 Mr Johnson asks Danny to write the number **four hundred and fifty two** in numerals. What does he write?

3 Imogen's teacher asks her to partition **929** into **hundreds**, **tens** and **ones**. How many **hundreds** are there?

4 If Zayne starts at the number **94** and keeps subtracting **10**, what is the smallest number he would reach on a **100** square?

5 Lucy partitions the number **128**. Show **two** ways that she could write this.

6 Carla thinks of a secret number. It is a multiple of **8**. The number is larger than **30** but smaller than **35**. What is Carla's number?

Solve mixed problems involving number and place value

1 Oscar has **34** stickers. He gives **10** to his friend, Amir. How many stickers does Oscar have left?

2 Shazad writes the number **143** in words. How does he write this?

3 There are **226** children eating their lunch. **100** children are having a packed lunch and the rest are having a school lunch. How many children are having a school lunch?

4 Sophia is making pancakes. She puts **200 g** of flour into a bowl. She then adds **6** more tablespoons of flour, each containing **10 g** of flour. How much flour is in the bowl now?

5 Leo partitions **985** in **two** different ways. How might he do this?

6 Look at the numbers below. What is the difference between the smallest and the largest number?

760   710   780   720   790

NUMBER

Addition and subtraction

These are all about addition and subtraction!

Add a three-digit number and ones (mentally)

1 George has **116** toy cars. For his birthday, he gets another **3**. How many toy cars does George have now?

2 Annie collects stamps. She has **250** and then gets **9** more. How many does she have now?

3 There are **105** boys and **7** girls in the football tournament. How many children are in the football tournament altogether?

4 Joe's football team have scored **123** goals so far this season. In the next **two** matches, they score **4** goals and **7** goals. How many goals have they scored altogether?

5 On Saturday, Sajid's takeaway sold **134** poppadoms. Bimaljeet then bought **5** and Kian bought another **7**. How many poppadoms have been sold now?

6 There are **117** grapes, **8** oranges, **9** bananas and **5** melons left in the fruit shop at the end of the day. How many pieces of fruit are left altogether?

Name ....

Subtract a three-digit number and ones (mentally)

1 Scarlett has **120** chocolate buttons. She eats **5**. How many buttons does she have left?

2 Evie thought of a number and added **8**. The answer was **128**. What was the number that she first thought of?

3 Adeeb has collected **172** football cards. This is **6** more than Robert. How many football cards has Robert collected?

4 Razia collected **147** badges. She gave **9** of them to her friend, Aimee. How many badges does Razia have left?

5 Mrs Patel has to drive **248** miles to get home. She drives **9** miles and then stops to buy a newspaper. She then drives another **7** miles and stops to buy petrol. How many more miles does she need to drive to get home?

6 There are **143** apples on the trees. The birds eat **9** and **8** more fall off the trees. How many apples are left on the trees?

Name ....

Add and subtract a three-digit number and ones (mentally)

1 Shani goes to the seaside and collects **120** pretty shells. She gives **9** of them to her mum. How many shells does Shani have left?

2 Florence builds a tower out of **232** bricks. **7** of the bricks are red and all the others are blue. How many bricks are blue?

3 Freddie thought of a number, then took away **5**. The answer was **127**. What was the number he thought of?

4 Georgia is at the aquarium. There are **378** little fish in a tank. In the same tank, she counts **9** big orange fish and **6** big blue fish. How many fish are in the tank altogether?

5 Arthur is given **103 pounds** for his birthday. He spends **£8** on a trip to the cinema. Then he buys a new t-shirt for **£9**. How much money does he have left?

Add a three-digit number and tens (mentally)

1 Britney can skip **122** times with her skipping rope, without stopping. Jenna can skip **20** more times than Britney without stopping. How many times can Jenna skip?

2 Katarina and Khalida go swimming every day for a week. Katarina swims **114** lengths and Khalida swims **30** lengths. How many lengths do they swim altogether?

3 In Frankie's Fruit Shop, there are **190** apples, and **20** pineapples. How many apples and pineapples are there altogether?

4 There are **17** children on the school bus. At the first stop, **20** children get on and at the second stop, another **10** children get on. How many children are on the bus now?

5 Janine was baking for a charity sale. She baked **123** chocolate biscuits, **80** plain biscuits and **40** cupcakes. How many biscuits and cakes did Janine bake altogether?

Subtract a three-digit number and tens (mentally)

1 Jack has **120** sweets. Joanna has **80** sweets. How many more sweets does Jack have than Joanna?

2 In the school hall, Mr Owen, the site supervisor, puts out **122** chairs for the Christmas Nativity Play. By 6 o'clock people are sitting on **30** chairs. How many chairs are empty?

3 Mrs Butler's garden has **138** sunflowers, but **50** die because of the bad weather. How many are left?

4 The zookeeper has **212** bananas in a big bag. The cheeky monkeys eat **90** bananas for breakfast. How many bananas are left for the monkeys' lunch?

5 Olga gets **104** Christmas cards altogether. She gets **70** from girls. How many cards are from boys?

6 In a cricket match, Oscar's team score **242** runs. Harriet's team score **90** runs. How many more runs did Oscar's team score than Harriet's team?

Name ....

Add and subtract a three-digit number and tens (mentally)

1 Amanda scored **102** on a maths test. Seb scored **90**. What is the difference between their scores?

2 Mrs Green grew **130** potatoes. She used **20** potatoes to make a shepherd's pie. How many potatoes does she have left?

3 Amber plants a sunflower and it grows to **120 cm**. Farah's sunflower grows **30 cm** taller. How tall is Farah's sunflower?

4 **143** people went on the school trip this year. This is **thirty** more than last year. How many people went on the school trip last year?

5 Harris is **90 cm** tall. His brother is **136 cm** tall. How much taller than Harris is his brother?

6 Matty has **103** red counters, **30** yellow counters and **80** blue counters. How many counters does Matty have altogether?

Name ....

Add a three-digit number and hundreds (mentally)

1 Loren counts **108** red cars and **100** blue cars. How many cars does she count in total?

2 Janek wants to build a tower. He has **125** red bricks and **200** blue bricks. How many bricks does he have altogether?

3 A basket has **137** strawberries. Another has **200**. How many strawberries are there altogether?

4 Mrs Bright asked Aslam to work out **138 + 200 + 300**. What answer should he give?

5 Riley scored **147** runs in a cricket match. Marlon and Kiera scored **300** runs between them. How many runs did Riley, Marlon and Kiera score altogether?

6 There are **178** sheep, **200** pigs, **100** cows and **400** chickens on the farm. How many animals are there on the farm altogether?

27

Name ....

Subtract a three-digit number and hundreds (mentally)

1 There are **350** pupils at Sunshine Primary School. Classes 3, 4 and 5 go on a trip to the theme park, leaving **200** children at school. How many children went on the trip to the theme park?

2 Kassia's team score **180** runs in a cricket match. Chloe's team score **100** runs. How many more runs do Kassia's team score than Chloe's?

3 Rebecca is reading a book. The book has **357** pages. She reads **200** pages. How many pages does she have left to read?

4 There are **180** bananas and **200** apples for the children at break. **300** pieces of fruit are eaten. How much fruit is left over?

5 There are **917** fiction books on the shelves in the library. On Monday, children take **200** away to read and on Wednesday, children take **400** away to read. How many books are left on the shelves?

Name ....

Add and subtract a three-digit number and hundreds (mentally)

1 Between 9 am and 5 pm a café sold **200** cups of coffee and **145** cups of tea. How many drinks did they sell altogether?

2 There are **328** sweets in a tub. Haima and Lucas eat **200** of the sweets. How many sweets are left?

3 Brannon and his grandad are making a cake. They start by putting **175 g** of sugar and **300 g** of butter into a bowl. How many **grams** of sugar and butter are in the bowl?

4 Yasmin is making necklaces. She has **762** beads. She uses **100** beads to make a necklace for her mum and **300** beads to make a necklace for her sister. How many beads does she have left?

5 Toby has **756** trading cards. Dexter has **300** and Layla has **100** cards. How many more trading cards does Toby have than Dexter and Layla put together?

29

Name ....

Add numbers with up to three digits using a formal written method

1 Complete the written method that Demi might use to calculate **42** add **88**.

$$
\begin{array}{r}
42 \\
+ \\
\hline
\end{array}
$$

2 Alicia collected **97** badges. Her mum bought her **45** more badges. How many badges does she have now?

3 There are **336** children and **45** staff at St Michael's Primary. How many people are in the school altogether?

4 How might Tabatha use a written method to add **423** to **87**? Show how she would set out the written method and then complete the calculation.

5 Miss Thompson wrote this problem on the whiteboard:

$$234 + 87 + 9 =$$

Use a written method of column addition to solve it.

Subtract numbers with up to three digits using a formal written method

1 Eloise has **£46** and she buys a new dress for **£12**. How much does she have left to buy some shoes? Set out your written method carefully and work out the answer.

2 Show how Josie might use a written method to calculate **96** subtract **32**. What is her answer?

3 Reuben solves **85** subtract **37** using a written method. How might he do it? What would his answer be?

4 How might Ava use a written method to subtract **48** from **396**? Show how she would do this and then write the answer.

5 Mr Berry writes this problem on the whiteboard:

505 - 166 =

Use a written method of column subtraction to solve it.

Add and subtract numbers with up to three digits using a formal written method

1 Stefan collected **265** conkers. He gave **52** of them to his friend, Mariam. How many conkers did Stefan have left? Use a written method to work out the answer.

2 How would Brandon use a written method to calculate **455** subtract **224**? What would his answer be?

3 Hamza used a written method to find the total of **154** and **286**. Show how you think he did it and then write the answer.

4 Suzi and Remy are members of a skiing club. Suzi has been a member for **657** days and Remy has been a member for **814** days. How many more days has Remy been a member than Suzi?

5 Asha is **126 cm** tall. Melissa is **117 cm** tall. Lydia is **137 cm** tall. What is the total of their heights?

Estimate the answer to a calculation

1 Niamh estimates that **11 + 18** would be about **30**. Is this a good estimation? Explain your answer.

2 Mrs Stone asks Jayne to estimate the answer to **48 + 52**. Circle the best estimation.

$$40 + 50 \qquad 50 + 50 \qquad 50 + 60$$

3 Mr Malik buys **4** packs of sweets. Each pack has **10** sweets. There are **36** children in his class. Will he have enough sweets to give to each child? Explain your answer.

4 There are **409** people at the cinema. If **311** people leave early, estimate, to the nearest **hundred**, how many people are left.

5 Tia is asked to subtract **196** from **303**. Use rounding to estimate the answer for Tia.

6 After rounding to the nearest **100**, Miss Bradley says there are **500** children in the school. What is the least number of children there could be in school?

Use inverse operations to check answers

1 Can you turn this number statement into a subtraction?

$$8 + 2 = 10$$

2 Mustafa says, "I can check my answer to **4 + 8 = 12** by subtracting **12** from **8**." Is Mustafa correct? Explain why?

3 Mr Mitchell wrote these calculations on the board. Can you fill in the missing numbers?

☐ + 8 = ☐   15 − 8 = 7

4 Esra works out that **9 + 7 = 16**. How could she check her answer using subtraction?

5 Hayley writes an inverse of **32 + 80 = 112**. What number statement might she write?

6 Skye checks her answer to **97 − 78 = 19** using the inverse. Show how she would do this?

Solve problems, including missing number problems, using number facts and place value

1 Danielle knows that **14 + 14 = 28**. Explain how she could use this fact to work out **14 + 15**.

2 If **half** of **36** is **18**, what is **double 18**?

3 Josh has a secret number. It is less than **20**, has **2** digits and is a multiple of **4**. The digits add up to **7**. What is Josh's number?

4 Sofia is selling her homemade orange juice. She squeezes **228** oranges on Monday, **193** on Tuesday and **277** on Wednesday. How many oranges has she used altogether?

5 Isla is trying to fill in the number statements by putting a number on each line. Can you help her complete the missing numbers?

| | - | 8 | = | 12 |

21 - | | = 13

| | - | | = 14

Solve addition money problems

1 On Saturday, Joseph's mum gives him **£1.30** and his dad gives him **45p**. How much does Joseph get altogether?

2 It costs **£1.24** to go swimming. How much would it cost Dominic and Shabana to go swimming together?

3 Mum buys Jessie and Mia an ice cream each. **One** ice cream costs **£1.55**. How much money does mum spend?

4 Grace buys a comic for **£1.80** and some new hair clips for **99p**. How much money does she spend in total?

Look at the cost of sweets in the shop and then answer Questions **5** and **6**.

Chewys - 17p	**Fruit Pops - 11p**	**Swirlys - 9p**
Frizzles - 15p	**Toffee Treats - 25p**	

5 Ebony buys a Frizzle, a Swirly and a Fruit Pop. How much does she spend?

6 Chloe has **50p**. Has she enough to buy **two** Frizzles and **one** Toffee Treat? Explain your answer.

Solve subtraction money problems

1 How much change does Cassie get from **67p** if she buys an apple from the fruit shop for **25p**?

2 Isabella has **£3.00**. She buys a gingerbread man for **75p**. How much money does she have left?

3 Jason has saved **£12.50**. He spends **£7.25** on a DVD. How much money does he have left?

4 For Eid, Rehana gets **£110**. She buys a game costing **£38**. How much will she have left?

5 Jayme has **£192**. He spends **£56** at the toy shop. Then he goes to the clothes shop and spends **£73**. How much does Jayme have left?

6 Max gets **£163** from all his family for his birthday. He buys a game for **£37**, a DVD Boxset for **£18** and he spends **£48** on a party. How much does he have left?

Solve addition and subtraction problems

1 There are **37** blue soft balls and **53** red soft balls in a play area. How many soft balls are there altogether in the play area?

2 Shabnum has **62p**. She gives Safraz **25p**. How much does Shabnum have left?

3 In Sarnie's Sandwich Shop, there are **13** cheese and tomato sandwiches, **25** turkey sandwiches and **14** ham sandwiches. Leon buys **2** turkey sandwiches and **1** ham sandwich. How many sandwiches are left in the shop?

4 In the PE hall, there are **275** bean bags. Mrs Clayton's class take **115**, Mr Thabani's class take **94** and Mrs England's class take **30**. How many bean bags are left?

5 Mario takes **86** oatmeal biscuits, **42** chocolate biscuits and **27** ginger biscuits to a party. At the end of the party, there were **39** biscuits left. How many biscuits have been eaten at the party?

6 Tilly thinks of a number. She adds **20** and subtracts **152**. The answer is **83**. What was her number?

Solve addition and subtraction problems

1 Monika thinks of a number then subtracts **15**. The answer is **30**. What was her number?

2 Rem has **88p** and Joshua has **47p**. What is the difference in the amount of money that they have?

3 Fergus scores **240** on a computer game. This is **82** more than Seth's score. What was Seth's score?

4 Mrs Anderson bought **250** bottles of water for her thirsty family. In June, they drank **57** bottles. In July, they drank **84** and in August, they drank **79**. How many bottles were left?

5 Class 3 recorded how many apples were sold in the school shop. Look at their results for week one.

Monday	Tuesday	Wednesday	Thursday	Friday
16	19	21	24	26

During week two, the shop sold **20** apples less than during week one. How many apples were sold in week two?

Solve addition and subtraction problems

1 Lok's favourite team has **48** points and his brother's favourite team has **39** points. How many points do the teams have in total?

2 Alice is saving up to buy some earrings for her mum's birthday. The earrings cost **£12**. Alice only has **£7.50**. How much more money does she need?

3 There are **258** people in the queue for the Big Bouncy Rollercoaster. **62** people leave the queue early because they are hungry. How many are still in the queue?

4 Taj thinks of a number, **doubles** it and adds **4**. His answer is **44**. What was Taj's number?

5 Sophia solves **984** minus **368** using a written method. Show how she might do this. What would her answer be?

6 On a farm, there are **340** chickens in a chicken coop. The farmer puts another **114** chickens into the coop. The farmer then takes **98** chickens from the coop to sell at the market. How many chickens are left?

NUMBER

Multiplication and division

These are all about multiplication and division!

Recall and use multiplication facts for the 3 times table

1 It costs **£3** to go swimming. How much would it cost for **4** children to go swimming?

2 There are **5** apples in a bag. How many apples would there be in **3** bags?

3 A toy car has **four** wheels. How many wheels would **three** toy cars have?

4 Mo can run **7** miles in an hour. How many miles could he run in **3** hours?

5 Harish has **3** toy sets with **10** dinosaurs in each set. How many dinosaurs are there altogether?

6 Dale got **80p** each week for his spending money. He saved this money for **3** weeks. How much did Dale save altogether?

Recall and use multiplication facts for the 4 times table

1 **Four** football cards come in a pack. Thomas buys **two** packs. How many cards does he have?

2 Duke, the dog, eats **3** Doggy Dinners every day. How many Doggy Dinners does he eat in **four** days?

3 Taxis hold **four** people. How many people would **4** taxis hold?

4 There are **10** carrots in a row in Mr Grime's garden. How many carrots are there in **4** rows?

5 Talha has a pack of **seven** colouring pencils. How many colouring pencils would he have if he had **four** packs?

6 Mr Fisher gives out **four** sweets to each child. He gives sweets out to **12** children. How many sweets does he give out altogether?

                   Name ....

Recall and use multiplication facts for the 8 times table

1 There are **8** chocolate biscuits in a pack. Mrs Piper buys **two** packs. How many biscuits has she bought?

2 Charlotte has **3** pots of daffodils. Each pot has **8** daffodils growing in it. How many daffodils are growing altogether?

3 Tam fills **6** boxes with **8** cupcakes in each box. How many cupcakes are there altogether?

4 In a netball competition, there are **eight** teams. Each team has **seven** players. How many players are there in total?

5 **One** spider has **8** legs. Aaron has **8** pet spiders. How many legs do the spiders have altogether?

6 Marianna likes to read **8** books a month. How many books would she read in a year?

Name ....

Recall and use multiplication facts for the 3, 4 and 8 times tables

1 There are **8** pens in a pack. Sienna buys **2** packs. How many pens does she buy altogether?

2 Mustafa is making dinner. He puts **3** potatoes on each plate. How many potatoes would he need for **4** plates?

3 Giraffes have **4** legs. There are **6** giraffes at the safari park. How many giraffe legs are there altogether?

4 There are **8** cereal bars in a packet. How many cereal bars do you have if you buy **8** packets?

5 Sarah rides her horse, Harry, **four** times a week. How many times does she go horse riding in **11** weeks?

6 Brad, Jay and Frankie have **12** football cards each. How many cards do they have altogether?

Recall and use multiplication facts for the 3, 4 and 8 times tables

1 **One** bag holds **4** tomatoes. How many tomatoes are in **2** bags?

2 Harvey builds a tower out of **8** bricks. How many bricks would he need to build **4** towers?

3 Mr Fowler eats chicken for his dinner **three** times a week. How many times does he eat chicken in **ten** weeks?

4 Mrs Edwards splits her class into **8** groups. Each group has **3** children. How many children are in her class?

5 At the One-Stop Pet Shop, there are **12** spiders. Each spider has **8** legs. How many spider legs are there altogether?

6 Helen, the hen, lays **3** eggs per week. Harriet, the hen, lays **4** eggs per week. In **7** weeks, how many eggs do Helen and Harriet lay altogether?

Name ....

Recall and use division facts for the 3 times table

1   Saima cooks **6** samosas. Saima and her brother eat the same amount of samosas and they eat all of them. How many samosas do they eat each?

2   There are **18** chocolates in a box. How many people can have **3** chocolates each?

3   There are **15** strawberries in a basket. Mr Murray shares them equally between his **3** children. How many strawberries do they have each?

4   Mr Bun, the baker, puts **3** chocolate drops on each cake. He uses **24** chocolate drops. How many cakes has he baked?

5   Mrs Grant has **3** daughters. She buys **27** bags of beads for necklace-making and shares them equally between her daughters. How many bags of beads do her daughters have each?

6   Jack has **36** mini eggs. He shares them equally between himself and his friends, Mohammad and Larissa. How many mini eggs will they get each?

Recall and use division facts for the 4 times table

1 Mina cuts her birthday cake into **8** pieces. She shares it between **4** friends. How many pieces of cake will they have each?

2 There are **12** biscuits in a packet. How many biscuits would **4** people get each?

3 Tia has **16** stickers to put in her sticker book. She can put **4** stickers on each page. How many pages will she use?

4 Mikey has **24** lemons. **4** lemons make a glass of lemonade. How many glasses of lemonade can Mikey make?

5 Ms Khan has **32** reading books in her class. She puts **4** books on each table. How many tables are in her class?

6 There are **48** children on the playground. Mr White puts the children in **4** equal lines. How many children are in each line? If **4** more children came onto the playground, how many would be in each line then?

Recall and use division facts for the 8 times table

1 Abby picks **16** daisies to make daisy chains. She makes each daisy chain with **8** daisies. How many daisy chains can she make?

2 There are **32** children in Year 3. Mr Parker, the teacher, divides his class into **8** groups. How many children are in each group?

3 **56** cars are in a car park. There are **8** cars on each level. How many levels are in the car park?

4 Miss Harper has picked **64** apples from the trees in her orchard. She put **8** apples in each basket. How many baskets did she need?

5 A fruit stall has **80** bananas. There are **10** bananas in each bunch. How many bunches of bananas are there?

6 The pet shop has **88** goldfish. There are **8** fish in each tank. How many fish tanks are there? How many fish would there be in **12** tanks?

Name ....

Recall and use division facts for the 3, 4 and 8 times tables

1 There are **9** ice pops in a box. **3** children share them equally. How many ice pops do they have each?

2 There are **16** bouncy balls in a box. They are given out to **8** children. How many bouncy balls does each child get?

3 Mrs Gardener grew **18** pumpkins. There are **3** pumpkins in each row. How many rows are there?

4 There are **32** roses in Mr Locke's garden. He gives his wife a bunch of **8** roses. How many more bunches of **8** roses can he make?

5 Kathryn needs to cook **48** pies. She puts **4** pies on each tray to cook. How many trays of pies will there be?

6 Imtiaz has **72** strawberries. To make **one** milkshake, he needs **8** strawberries. How many strawberry milkshakes could he make with all the strawberries?

Recall and use division facts for the 3, 4 and 8 times tables

1 There were **12** dolls in the toy box. The dolls were shared between **4** children. How many dolls did they have each? 3 ✓

2 **Three** eggs are needed to make a cake. Paul has **twelve** eggs. How many cakes could he make? 4 ✓

3 Mr Akhtar shares **£28** between his **4** sons. How much money do they get each? £7 50p

4 Freya bakes **36** jam tarts for her party guests. She gives them **3** each. How many guests are given jam tarts? 12 ✓

5 Sakiya has **72** printed photographs. She puts them into a photo album. Each page holds **8** photographs. How many pages does she use? 9

6 Michael, Dave, Charlotte, and Clara share **48** sweets. How many sweets do they get each? 12 ✓

Recall and use multiplication and division facts for the 3, 4 and 8 times tables

1 Mrs Lawson drives her car **3** times a day. How many times does she drive her car in **4** days? 12

2 Mum bought **20** cartons of apple juice. There are **4** cartons in a box. How many boxes did mum buy? 5

3 If **24** children are divided into **three** teams, how many children are in each team? 8

4 Jacob is decorating cakes. He has **36** jelly sweets. He puts **4** sweets on each cake. How many cakes can he decorate? 9

5 Tara saves **64** pounds for her holiday to Scotland. She divides the money equally between the **8** days she is there. How much money does she have for each day? 8

10 × 4 = 40

6 Maddy thinks of a number and multiplies it by **4**. The answer is **52**. What was her number? 13

Recall and use multiplication and division facts for the 3, 4 and 8 times tables

1 Alex has **3** tubes of sweets. Each tube has **8** sweets. How many sweets does he have? 24 ✓

2 John is collecting money for charity. He collects **£4** each day for **10** days. How much money does he collect altogether? £40 ✓

3 Year 3 planted poppies in the school garden. They planted **6** rows of **8** seeds. How many poppies did Year 3 plant? 48 ✓

4 **28** biscuits are shared equally between **four** tables in Miss Thompson's class. How many biscuits are put on each table? 7 ✓

5 Saghir is saving up for some new trainers. He saves **£3** each week for **12** weeks. How much money does Saghir save? £36 ✓

6 Harish has **36** football cards. He puts them into **6** equal piles. How many football cards does he put in each pile? 6 ✓

Solve problems involving doubling and connecting the 2, 4 and 8 times tables

1 Josh knows his **2** times table but not his **4** times table. Explain, using numbers or words, how he can solve **4 x 4** using his **2** times table.

2 Natasha knows that **2 x 4** is **8**. How could she use this to help her work out **2 x 8**? Explain your answer using numbers or words.

3 There are **8** people on the bus. **8** more people get on the bus. How many people are on the bus altogether? Work this out using the **2** times tables.

4 Mr Khan has banned the **8** times table in his class. He asks Molly to work out **8 x 8** by using the **4** times table. Explain how she could do this.

5 Latishya has **6** tubs, each containing **8** buttons. How many buttons does she have altogether? Use your knowledge of the **4** times table to help you. Explain how you found your answer.

Solve problems involving multiplication of a two-digit number by a one-digit number, using a mental method

1. A box of chocolates has **12** chocolates on each layer. There are **4** layers in a box. How many chocolates are there in the box altogether? 48 ✓

2. Imran swims **8** lengths of a **10 metre** pool. How many **metres** does he swim in total? 80 ✓

3. Lauren buys **5** apples for **24p** each. How much does she spend? £1.20p ✓

4. Jasmine has **23** friends coming to her birthday party and she wants to make sure they have **3** cup cakes each. How many cupcakes will she need to bake? 69 ✓

5. There are **44** people on the aeroplane. Each person has **3** items of luggage. How many items of luggage are there altogether? 132 ✓

6. Charlotte has **4** jars with **53** marbles in each jar. How many marbles does Charlotte have altogether? 212 ✓

Solve problems involving multiplication of a two-digit number by a one-digit number, using a mental method

1 In assembly, there are **8** children in each row. There are **12** rows. How many children are there in assembly? *96* ✓

2 Usman is building lego towers. To build **one** tower, he needs **38** pieces of lego. How many pieces does he need to build **2** lego towers? *76* ✓

3 If **30** children have **five** reading books each, how many books do they have altogether? *150* ✓

$$20 \times 4 = 80$$
$$6 \times 4 = 24$$

$$120 \quad 24$$
$$5 \times 30 =$$

4 Dana got **£26** each week from working at the café on Saturday. She saved this money for **4** weeks. How much did Dana save? *£144* ✗

10 4

5 **27** children put **five** Christmas cards each into the Christmas post box. How many cards were in the post box altogether? *135* ✓

6 Dad has been saving coins. He has **6** jars with **28** coins in each jar. How many coins does he have in total? *168*

$$6 \times 20 = 120$$
$$6 \times 8$$

Solve problems involving division of a two-digit number by a one-digit number, using a mental method

1 There are **72** grapes in a bag. How many people can have **8** grapes each?

2 Cameron has **24** t-shirts. His mum asks him to share them equally between **3** drawers in his dressing table. How many t-shirts does he put in each drawer?

3 Shogusta has **60p**. She shares it equally between herself, Safraz and Connor. How much do they get each?

4 A big box of biscuits has **75** biscuits in **5** layers. How many biscuits are in each layer?

5 Tara thinks of a number and multiplies it by **4**. Her answer is **160**. What was her number?

6 Mum puts **£45** in a tin and Dad adds another **£20**. They share the money equally between their **five** children. How much does each child get?

Name ....

Solve problems involving division of a two-digit number by a one-digit number, using a mental method

1 In Miss Harris' class, there are **28** children. She divides her class into **2** groups. How many children are in each group?

2 A taxi can carry **4** people. How many taxis would be needed to take **32** people to the One Destination music concert?

3 Perry's Pet Shop keeps **5** stick insects in each tank. How many tanks would be needed for **75** stick insects?

4 There are **96** bananas for break time. **3** classes each get an equal amount. How many bananas does each class get?

5 At the theme park, the Tummy Tickler ride takes **8** people at a time. How many rides are needed so that **96** people can have a turn?

6 Alex has **96** sweets, shared equally between **4** bags. If he eats **3** sweets from each bag, how many sweets would be in each bag then?

Solve problems involving multiplication using a formal written method

(For each of the problems show your written method.)

1 In the furniture store, each table has **4** legs. How many legs would **22** tables have? *88*

2 Miss Jones asks Kai to work out **24** multiplied by **3**. Show how he would do this. *8* how many 3's go into 24

3 There are **52** cards in a pack. How many cards are there in **5** packs? *~~268~~* *260* ✓

4 In the theatre, there are **8** rows of **17** chairs. How many chairs are there altogether in the theatre? *136*

5 One Tongue Twister sweet costs **16p**. Aidan buys **one** for himself and his **7** friends. How much does he spend? *42 p*

6 Which is more: **24** multiplied by **8** or **46** multiplied by **4**? Show your written multiplication method for both calculations. 2nd one

48/12, 16, 20, 24, 28, 32, 36 49   192

Solve problems involving division using a formal written method

(For each of the problems show your written method.)

1 How many teams of **4** can be made from **84** people?

2 A group of **56** children are going to the fair. They are travelling in cars. **4** children can fit into each car. How many cars are needed for the trip?

3 A pizza serves **3** hungry children. How many pizzas would be needed to feed **72** hungry children?

4 The miniature steam train holds **8** people at a time, for a circuit of the track. How many times would the train have to go round the track if **96** people wanted a ride?

5 Edward is giving out coloured pencils. He gives **8** pencils to each person. Edward has **99** pencils to give out. How many people are given coloured pencils? How many coloured pencils would be left over?

Solve problems involving multiplication and division using a formal written method

(For each of the problems show your written method.)

1 Mr Patel gives each of his **four** sons **£16**. How much does he give to his sons altogether?

2 How many teams of **3** can be made from **39** people?

3 In the PE cupboard, there are **94** bean bags. Ms Bluebell gives out the bean bags to **8** groups. How many bean bags do each group get? How many bean bags are left over?

4 Use a formal written method to work out **26** multiplied by **3**.

5 Hina swims **46** lengths a week. How many lengths does she swim in **8** weeks?

6 In a week at the zoo, **97** fish are shared betweeen **3** penguins. There are some fish left over. How many fish does each penguin get and how many are left over?

Solve multiplication problems, including scaling and correspondence problems

1 Tom's dad is making Tom a tree house. Firstly, he makes a model of the tree house which is **50 cm** high. When the tree house is made, it is **eight** times as high as the model. How high is the real tree house?

2 Coco The Clown has **14** different red noses and **4** different wigs. How many different clown outfits can he wear?

3 Grumpy the Giant is **14 metres** tall. Jack is **ten** times smaller than Grumpy. How tall is Jack?

4 Megan made a huge ice cube that weighed **720 grams**. In the 3 hours after it was taken out of the freezer, it shrank by **8** times its original size. How heavy was the ice cube after 3 hours?

5 Mr Potato Head has **13** different noses and **8** different mouths. How many different Mr Potato Heads can be made?

NUMBER

Fractions

These are all about fractions!

Recognise that tenths arise from dividing an object into 10 equal parts

1 Utaka eats $\frac{1}{10}$ of her pizza. How many **tenths** are left?

2 Jake has **10** cars. He gives **2** to his brother. What fraction of cars does Jake have left?

3 Hollie has **10** DVDs. She watches **3** with her mum. Write the number of DVDs they have watched as a fraction.

4 Charlotte's birthday cake is cut into **10** pieces. If **6** children at her party have a piece, what fraction of the cake is left?

5 Woody, the woodcutter, cuts a piece of wood into **10** pieces. He uses **7** pieces of wood to make a chair. Write as a fraction how many pieces are left.

6 Lily-May eats **3 tenths** of her birthday cake. Her sister eats **2 tenths** of the cake. How much birthday cake have they eaten? Write your answer as a fraction.

Recognise, find and write unit fractions of a discrete set of objects

1 **One half** of an orange has **8** segments. How many segments would there be in a whole orange? 10

2 There are **12** sheep in a field. **One quarter** of the sheep are eating grass. How many sheep are not eating grass? 9

3 Hazel has **15** teddies. She gives $\frac{1}{3}$ of her teddies to her little sister, Megan. How many teddies has she given to Megan? 5

4 Terri has **30** books. She puts her books in piles. Each pile is a **sixth** of the total amount. How many books are in each pile? 5

5 Mikey's bar of chocolate had **24** pieces. He wanted to break the bar into **eighths**. How many pieces would be in each **eighth**? 8

6 A premiership football costs **£18** in the sale. It is $\frac{1}{3}$ of the original price. How much was the football originally? 5 4

Recognise, find and write non-unit fractions of a discrete set of objects

1 Chantelle has **15** dresses in her wardrobe. $\frac{2}{3}$ of her dresses are pink. How many of Chantelle's dresses are pink?

2 Jayden had **40** football cards. He wanted to find out how many cards would make up **three quarters** of his collection. Explain how Jayden would work this out. What would his answer be?

3 Mrs Dewhurst bakes **27** miniature apple pies. Her family eat $\frac{2}{3}$ of them. How many pies are left?

4 Sadie has **30** fizzy sweets. She eats **three fifths** of her fizzy sweets. How many sweets has she eaten?

5 Stevie had **54** DVDs. He sold **five sixths** of his collection. How many DVDs did he sell?

Understand equivalence in unit and non-unit fractions

1 The twins, Atlanta and Phoenix, were sharing a cake. Atlanta had **half** of the cake and Phoenix had **two quarters**. Did they have the same amount? Explain your answer.

2 Edul cuts a cake into **6** equal slices. He eats **2** slices of his cake. Has Edul eaten $\frac{1}{2}$ of his cake? Explain your answer.

3 Billy ordered a pizza. The pizza chef asked if he would like the pizza cutting into **quarters** or **eighths**. Billy said, "Just into **quarters**, because I'm hungry enough to eat **4** pieces, but not hungry enough to eat **8** pieces." Explain why Billy's answer didn't make sense.

4 There are **50** marbles in a box. Marcus takes **two tenths** of the marbles. Caitlin takes $\frac{1}{5}$ of the marbles. Do they have the same amount of marbles?

5 Reece has saved **£6**. He says, "If I spend **two thirds** of my money, that's the same as spending **three sixths** of my money." Is he correct? Explain your answer.

Understand the relation between unit fractions as operators and division by integers

1 Gabi had **20** sweets. She wanted to share the sweets between herself and **3** friends by finding a **quarter** of the sweets. How many would each person have?

2 Kamran has **30** iced cakes. He gives them out equally to himself and **5** friends by working out $\frac{1}{6}$ of the cakes. How many would each person have?

3 Mr Redmond has **24** pots of paint. He shares them between **8** children. He does this by finding **one eighth** of the paint pots. How many pots of paint would each child have?

4 Tyrone works out that **70 ÷ 5 = 14**. What is **one fifth** of **70**?

5 Mrs Jameson asks her class work out a **sixth** of **42** and a **fifth** of **60** and then add the **two** answers together. Explain using words or numbers how you would do this. Write the answer too.

Name ....

Add fractions with the same denominator within one whole

1 Mrs Holden asks her class what $\frac{1}{3}$ add $\frac{1}{3}$ would be. What answer should they give?

2 Jordan drinks $\frac{1}{4}$ of his bottle of juice with his lunch. He then drinks another $\frac{2}{4}$ of his juice. How much of his juice has Jordan drunk altogether? Give your answer as a fraction.

3 Lewis ate **two fifths** of his chocolate bar at lunchtime. He ate another $\frac{2}{5}$ on the way home. What fraction of his chocolate bar did he eat altogether?

4 Amelie runs $\frac{3}{7}$ of her way home from school. She then walks $\frac{2}{7}$ more. What fraction of the distance has she travelled altogether?

5 **Two eighths** of Farmer Fred's cows are moved to field A. Farmer Fred then moves another $\frac{5}{8}$ of his cows to field A. Write the fraction of cows that are in field A now.

Subtract fractions with the same denominator within one whole

1. Carrie needs to subtract $\frac{1}{3}$ from $\frac{2}{3}$. What would her answer be?

2. $\frac{4}{5}$ of the herd of elephants were cooling down in the water. $\frac{2}{5}$ of the elephants then get out the water to find food. What fraction of the elephants are left in the water?

3. **Three quarters** of Year 3 are playing outside. $\frac{1}{4}$ of Year 3 go back inside to their classroom. What fraction of Year 3 are still outside?

4. $\frac{5}{6}$ of Logan's cupcakes are iced with either blue or red icing. $\frac{2}{6}$ of his cakes have red icing. What fraction of his cupcakes have blue icing?

5. Faisal eats $\frac{5}{8}$ of his chocolate bar and gives **two eighths** of his chocolate bar to his brother. How much chocolate does he have left?

68

Name ....

Add and subtract fractions with the same denominator within one whole

1 Mo adds $\frac{1}{4}$ and $\frac{2}{4}$. What is his answer?

2 Talia took $\frac{1}{3}$ of the pencils from the box. Michael took another **third** of the pencils from the box. What fraction of the pencils did Talia and Michael take out altogether?

3 Simone is trying to work out what $\frac{2}{6}$ add **three sixths** would be. What fraction should she write?

4 Mr Jenson takes $\frac{4}{5}$ of the school bean bags from the bean bag box. He gives out **three fifths** to his class. What fraction of bean bags does he have left?

5 Pete walks his dog, Deefer, $\frac{2}{5}$ of the way around the park. They have a rest and then walk another $\frac{2}{5}$ of the way around the park. What fraction do Pete and Deefer still need to walk to go the whole way around the park?

6 Matty spends $\frac{3}{8}$ of his money on a t-shirt. He then buys a magazine with $\frac{1}{8}$ of his money. His grandma gives him $\frac{2}{8}$ of his money back. How much money does he have now? Write your answer as a fraction.

69 Name ....

Compare and order unit fractions and non-unit fractions with the same denominator

1 Mr Badal asks his class which fraction is bigger: $\frac{3}{4}$ or $\frac{2}{4}$. Which one should they choose?

2 Bubbles, the cat, ate **two thirds** of her food. Growler, the dog, ate $\frac{1}{3}$ of his food. Which pet ate the larger fraction of their food?

3 Jess had **one fifth** of the bottle of cola and Jake had **two fifths** of the bottle. Who had more? Explain your answer.

4 Tyler had $\frac{2}{6}$ of the pizza, James had $\frac{1}{6}$ and Caitlin had $\frac{3}{6}$. Who had the most and who had the least?

5 Put these fractions in order of size, starting with the smallest:

3/8   4/8   1/8   7/8

Name ....

Solve problems involving fractions

1 Victoria has a **200 ml** glass of milk. She drinks **half** of it. How many **millilitres** of milk does she have left?

2 Edward wants to find $\frac{1}{4}$ of **£20**. What would his answer be in **pounds**?

3 Ruby has **25** sweets. **One fifth** of them are chewy. How many chewy sweets does Ruby have?

4 There are **30** children in a class. $\frac{2}{3}$ of the class are girls. How many boys are there in the class?

5 A shop had **12 kilograms** of apples. They sold $\frac{5}{6}$ of the apples on Tuesday. How many **kilograms** of apples did the shop have left?

6 Would you prefer to have $\frac{1}{2}$ of **£24** or $\frac{1}{4}$ of **£36**?

Solve problems involving fractions

1 Dom ate $^4/_8$ of his pizza on Monday night. On Tuesday, he ate another $^3/_8$. What fraction of his pizza did he eat on Monday and Tuesday altogether?

2 Mrs Bunter cut her cake into **6** equal pieces. She gave her daughter, Farah, **2** pieces. What fraction of the cake did Farah have?

3 Zav has **one half** of the play dough. Ricky has **two quarters**. Who has the most play dough? Explain your answer.

4 If **60 ÷ 5 = 12**, what is **one twelfth** of **60**?

5 Nita says, "A **quarter** of the numbers on a **hundred** square are even." Is she correct and how do you know?

6 In the shop 'Look Beautiful', a dress has been reduced by **one eighth**. It was **£32**. How much is it now?

Name ....

Solve problems involving fractions

1 Marlon is trying to work out how many **tenths** are shaded. Can you help him?

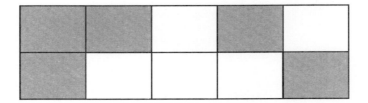

2 Marlon then completes the shading on the shape so that **eight tenths** of the shape are shaded. Shade the shape to show how Marlon might have done it.

3 Gemma has worked out that **4** divided by **10** is **0.4**. What would the answer be to **5** divided by **10**?

4 There are **8** horses in a field. **5** of the horses are eating grass and the rest are galloping around the field. What fraction of the horses are galloping?

5 Mrs Williams asks her class to choose a fraction that is the same as $\frac{1}{8}$. Can you name **2** fractions that they could choose?

6 A pair of trainers has a **quarter** off the price in the sale. If they cost **£48** before the sale, how much are they in the sale?

Name ....

MEASUREMENT

These are all about measurement!

Solve problems involving comparing lengths

1 Chen had a stick of seaside rock measuring **23 cm** in length. Paul's stick of rock was **32 cm**. Whose piece of rock was longer?

2 Tom's stick measures **45.5 cm**. Farouk's stick measures **44.5 cm**. Whose stick is longer?

3 Kelsie's hand span measures **8.5 centimetres**. Harriet's hand span measures **86 millimetres**. Who has the wider hand span?

4 The height of the dining room door is **2.25 metres**. The height of the kitchen door is **2 metres 30 cm**. Which door is taller?

5 Ollie is **124 cm** tall. Georgie is **1 metre 16 cm** tall. Who is taller?

6 Sharrin's sunflower grew **1.2 metres** in the month of May. In June, the sunflower grew **115 cm**. In July, the sunflower grew **0.9 m**. In which month did Sharrin's sunflower grow the most and in which month did it grow the least?

Solve problems involving comparing mass (weight)

1 Kim's chocolate bar weighs **80 grams**. Tyler's chocolate bar weighs **75 grams**. Whose chocolate bar is heavier?

2 Violet is making biscuits. She puts **180 g** of flour into a red bowl and **120 g** of flour into a blue bowl. Which bowl is heavier?

3 A glass-top table in the furniture store weighs **86.5 kilograms**. A wooden table weighs **85.6 kilograms**. Which table is heavier?

4 Greg weighs **46.4 kilograms**. His dad weighs **64.4 kilograms**. Who is heavier?

5 Tommy, the tiger, weighs **202 kilograms**. Talia, his tigress, weighs **200,000 grams**. Who is heavier?

6 Mrs Jackson's handbag weighs **1.2 kg**. Miss Denby's bag weighs **1250 grams**. Mrs Whitford's bag weighs **1.3 kg**. Whose bag is the heaviest and whose bag is the lightest?

Solve problems involving comparing capacity

1 Demi has a glass containing **78 ml** of orange juice. Rachel has a glass containing **87 ml** of orange juice. Whose glass contains more orange juice?

2 Jason buys a **2.5 litre** bottle of cola. Lisa buys a bottle containing **2.75 litres** of cola. Who has more cola?

3 The red jug holds **500 millilitres** of water. The green jug holds **0.6 litres** of water. Which jug has the bigger capacity?

4 At the aquarium, there are **425 litres** of water in Fish Tank A. Fish Tank B has **452 litres** of water. Which tank has more water?

5 Frankie has a jug filled with **1200 ml** of orange juice. Nick has **1 litre 25 ml** of orange juice in his jug. Who has more orange juice?

6 Kyle's paddling pool is filled with **93,000 millilitres** of water. Adam's paddling pool is filled with **94 litres** of water. Zara's paddling pool is filled with **92,000 millitres** of water.   Whose pool has the most and whose pool has the least water?

76

Name ....

Solve problems involving comparing length, mass and capacity

1 In Mr Thackeray's garden, the green barrel can hold **67 litres** of rainwater. The brown barrel can hold **76 litres** of rainwater. Which barrel has the bigger capacity of water?

2 Anna weighs **42.5 kilograms**. Her mum weighs **45.2 kilograms**. Who is heavier?

3 A garden has **two** fences. Fence **A** is **38 m** and Fence **B** is **3900 cm**. Which fence is longer?

4 The distance from Netherton to Brigley is **48 km**. The distance from Netherton to Hoxley is **49,000 m**. Which town is further from Netherton?

5 Reuben walked to school every morning. If he walked past the shops, the distance was **221 m**. If he walked past the park, the distance was **212 m**. Which was the shorter way to school? How much shorter?

6 Aden is **110 cm** tall, Lennie is **1.2 metres** tall and Josh is **1356 mm** tall. Who is the tallest and who is the shortest?

Solve problems involving adding and subtracting lengths

1 Sammy threw his ball **5 metres**. Then he threw it another **4 metres**. How far did Sammy throw the ball altogether? Convert your answer to **centimetres**.

2 Wilma is **125 cm** tall. Over the year she grows **16 cm**. How tall is Wilma now?

3 The bathroom window is **66 cm** long. The bedroom window is **93 cm** long. How much longer is the bedroom window than the bathroom window?

4 Eduardo is **1 m 42 cm** tall. His sister Sasha is **23 cm** shorter. How tall is Sasha?

5 On Thursday, Barry The Builder built a wall **53 m** long. On Friday, he built another **17 m** of wall. On Saturday, a truck accidentally knocked down **23 metres** of the wall. How many **metres** of wall were left?

6 A paper chain measures **365 cm** and another paper chain measures **257 cm**. The two paper chains are joined together to make a new one. How much longer than **6 metres** is the new paper chain?

Solve problems involving adding and subtracting mass (weight)

1 A comic weighs **50 grams** and Callum buys **2** comics. What is the weight of both comics?

2 Janine has **58 grams** of sweets in a paper bag. She eats **23 grams** of the sweets. What weight of sweets does she have left?

3 Safron's empty pencil case weighs **35 grams**. Safron puts in a pencil sharpener which weighs **25 grams** and a pencil which weighs **15 grams**. What is the weight of the pencil case now?

4 To make **2** cakes, Jamie needs **110 g** of flour, **55 g** of butter and **50 g** of sugar. What is the weight of all **3** ingredients added together?

5 Alice and her mum and dad are going on holiday on a plane. Alice's case weighs **23 kg**. Her mum's case weighs **24 kg** and her dad's case weighs **28 kg**. The weight limit for each case is **20 kg**. How much over the total weight limit are the **3** cases altogether?

6 To bake **one** loaf of bread, Zane needs **350 grams** of flour. He buys **1 kilogram** of flour. How many loaves of bread can he bake? How much flour will he have left?

79

Name ....

Solve problems involving adding and subtracting capacity

1 There are **100 millilitres** of milk left in the bottle. Josh pours **70 millilitres** onto his cereal. How much milk is left?

2 Mrs Johnson is making a cup of tea. She puts in the tea bag then pours **200 ml** of hot water into her cup. She then adds **30 ml** of milk. How many **millilitres** are in the cup altogether?

3 Mena pours **25 ml** of cordial into a glass. She then adds **75 ml** of water. How much is in the glass altogether?

4 Daisy bought **6.5 litres** of fizzy drink for her party. At the end of the party, she had **2 litres** left. How many **litres** of fizzy drink were drunk at her party?

5 Mrs Iqbal has **55 litres** of petrol in her car. She uses **20 litres** and then puts in another **15 litres**. How much petrol is in the car now?

6 The corner shop sold **7 litres** of lemonade in the morning and **10 litres** in the afternoon. There were **6 litres** left. How many **litres** did the shop have to begin with?

Solve problems involving adding and subtracting length, mass and capacity

1 A sunflower was **75 centimetres** tall. It grew **9 centimetres** in a month. How tall is the sunflower now?

2 Britney has a **500 ml** bottle of juice. She drinks **200 ml**. How much juice does she have left?

3 Mrs Davies is **1.53 metres** tall. She puts a hat on which makes her **9 cm** taller. How tall is she with the hat on?

4 Cole travels **62 km** by coach, **35 km** by taxi and then he walks for **5 km**. How far does he travel in total?

5 Mr Wilson's class are building a fence for Floppy, the class rabbit. The fence needs to be **385 cm** long. On the first day, they build **140 cm**. On the second day, they build another **125 cm**. How many more **centimetres** do they need to build?

6 Lucy, Raluca and Dylan were doing a sponsored walk. Lucy walked **3500 metres**. Raluca walked **3.5 kilometres**. Dylan walked **2500 metres**. How far did they walk altogether? Give your answer in **kilometres**.

Solve problems involving adding and subtracting length, mass and capacity

1 Rachel throws a ball for her dog, Milo. She throws it **27 metres**. Katie throws the ball **23 metres** for Milo. How far did they throw the ball together?

2 Aaron is **126 cm** tall. Corban is **15 cm** smaller than Aaron. How tall is Corban?

3 Brooklyn has a **1 litre** bottle of water. He drinks **375 ml**. How much water does he have left?

4 Shamin's plant grew to a height of **500 millimetres**. Tahera's plant grew to a height of **53 centimetres** and Linton's grew to **67 centimetres**. What is the difference in height, in **centimetres**, between the shortest and tallest plant?

5 Mr Waddington's class are building a **375 cm** tower from cereal boxes. After the first day, it was **128 cm** tall. On the second day, they built another **112 cm**. How many more **centimetres** of the tower do they need to build?

6 Janine weighed out **1.2 kg** of sugar onto the scales. She added **550 g** of flour. How many **grams** of sugar and flour were on the scales altogether?

Add amounts of money and work out change

1 Hannah has **£1.40**. Her mum gives her **50p**. How much money does she have now?

2 Jav has **four £1** coins and **seven 5p** coins. How much does he have altogether?

3 William buys **4** jam doughnuts for **60p** each. How much change does he get from **£3.00**?

4 Henry buys a sandwich for **£1.20** and a biscuit for **45p**. How much change does he get from **£2.00**?

School Fair Prices	
Key ring - **£1.60**	Ball - **£1.20**
Game - **£2.00**	Pen & pencil set - **£1.70**

5 Youlanda has **£5.00**. She buys a ball and a game. How much change does she have?

6 Tiffany spends **£4.50** on **3** items. What are they?

83

Name ....

Subtract amounts of money and work out change

1 Archie has **90p**. He spends **30p** on a bag of crisps. How much money does he have left?

2 Helena has **£1.00**. She spends **65p** on an ice cream at Mr Frosty's ice cream van. How much change will she receive?

3 Tessa has **£20**. She buys a new jumper for **£9**. She then buys a headband for **£3**. How much money does she have left?

4 Mr Jones bought **2** plants for his garden. Each plant cost **£1.50**. How much change did he get from **£5**?

5 In a restaurant, Toffee Dessert costs **£1.75** and Fruit Dessert costs **£2.15**. Alana has a Toffee Dessert and Demi has a Fruit Dessert. How much change will they have from **£5.00**?

6 Roxanne has **£5**. A basket of strawberries costs **£1.30**. Does Roxanne have enough to buy **4** baskets? Explain your answer.

Name ....

Add and subtract money to give amounts of change

1 Claudia has **£2.00**. She buys a bracelet for **£1.00**. How much money does she have left?

2 Amina has **£1.40**. Her grandma gives her **50p**. How much money does she have altogether?

3 Jake has **£1.20**. He wins another **£1.30** playing a fairground game. How much does he have now?

4 Kebabs cost **£1.45** each. Kai buys **one** and pays with a **£2** coin. How much change does he get?

5 What is the total cost of a cupcake costing **35p**, an apple costing **15p** and a drink costing **40p**?

6 Javeen has saved **three 50p** coins and **four 20p** coins. How much has she saved in total?

7 Leo has **four £1** coins, **two 20p** coins and **one 10p** coin. He then spends **50p** on a drink. How much money does he have left?

Name ....

Add and subtract money to give amounts of change

1 Chelsea has **105p** and Jay has **150p**. How much money, in **pence**, have they got altogether?

2 Joelle's mum gives her **three £1** coins, **two 5p** coins and **six 10p** coins. How much does Joelle's mum give her altogether?

3 Victoria has **two 50p** coins and **five 20p** coins. Her favourite magazine costs **£1.70**. How much change does she get?

4 Look at the cost of rides at the Funky Fairground:

Big Dipper - **90p**   Dodgems - **80p**
Space Stroller - **£1.20**   Twister - **70p**
Big Wheel - **£1.30**   Ghost Train - **50p**

How much would it cost to go on the Twister and the Space Stroller?

5 Serena has **£2**. She goes on **more than one** ride and does not get any change. Which rides could Serena have gone on?

Record and compare time in terms of seconds, minutes and hours and o'clock

1 It took Jez just **two minutes** to score his first goal of the match. How many **seconds** was this?

2 Paul ran one lap of the track in **3 minutes**. Mason ran one lap in **190 seconds**. Who was faster? By how many **seconds**?

3 Daryl went swimming for **one hour**. Kylie went swimming for **60 minutes**. Did they go swimming for the same amount of time? Explain your answer.

4 The train journey to the seaside took **2 hours**. How many **minutes** did the journey take?

5 Imran and Nicole went to the cinema but watched different films. Imran's film lasted **one hour, forty five minutes**. Nicole's film started at **6.40 pm** and lasted until **8.15 pm**. Whose film was longer? Explain your answer.

6 The aeroplane to Greece took off at **1 o'clock** and landed at **5 o'clock**. How many minutes did the flight take?

Use vocabulary such as am/pm, morning, afternoon, evening, noon and midnight

1 Mrs Harris went to the shops at **11 am**. She came home at **1 pm**. Did she arrive home in the morning or in the afternoon?

2 Carrie went fishing at **2 o'clock** in the afternoon. She told her mum that she would be back by **5 am** on the same day. Why was this impossible?

3 Uzma is going on holiday. She needs to wake up at **4 am**. She thinks she will be getting up in the afternoon. Is she correct? Explain your answer.

4 Louisa has a picnic at **12 noon**. Her friend, Gemma, says that it will be dark at that time. Is Gemma correct? Explain your answer.

5 Sebastian is going to a party at **6 pm**. He tells his mum he will be back at **9 am** that evening. Is he correct? Explain your answer.

6 What time is it **12 hours** later than **12 noon**?

Know the number of seconds in a minute

1 Jake held his breath for **one minute**. How many **seconds** was this?

2 Jess wanted to skip for **one minute** without stopping. If she had already skipped for **45 seconds**, how many more **seconds** did she need to skip for?

3 Year 3 were catching the bus to the swimming pool in **2 minutes**. How many **seconds** did they have to wait to catch the bus?

4 **90 seconds** were added on to the end of the match as additional time. How many **minutes** was this?

5 Demi's mum said she had to go to bed in **5 minutes**. How many **seconds** did she have left to stay up?

6 Which is longer: **240 seconds** or **3 minutes**? Explain your answer.

Know the number of days in each month

1 How many **days** are there in **January**?

2 Which has more **days**: **September** or **July**?

3 Put the months below in order starting from the month with the least **days**, to the month with the most.

   May   **February**   **November**

4 Bartek was going on a long trip for all of **April** and **May**. How many **days** was he going for altogther?

5 How many **days** are in **February** and **March** altogether, if it is a leap year?

6 How many **days** are there altogether in **June**, **July**, **August** and **September**?

Know the number of days in a year and a leap year

1   Noor went running every day for **one year** (not a leap year). For how many **days** did Noor go running?

2   It's Jasmine's birthday on the **29th February**. How many **years** will it be until she next celebrates her birthday on the **29th February**?

3   How many **days** are there in a **leap year**?

4   In 2015 (not a leap year), Giuseppe lived in England but went to Italy to stay with his cousins for **June** and **July**. For how many **days** was Giuseppe in England during 2015?

5   How many **days** are there in **July**, **August** and **October** altogether?

6   Layla lives in England but, in 2015, she went on holiday to Australia for **6 weeks**. How many **days** was Layla in England during 2015?

Calculate the time taken by particular events

1 In a race, Katie ran **2** laps of the school field. It took her **two minutes**. How many **seconds** did it take her?

2 Marnie and Sarah went swimming at **12 noon**. They stayed in the pool for **two hours**. What time did they finish swimming?

3 The time on the clock showed **11:15**. The correct time was **11:21**. How many **minutes** slow was the clock?

4 Josie goes running at **3:30 pm**. She runs for **40 minutes**. What time does she finish running?

5 School lunch lasts for **1 hour 10 minutes**. It ends at **1:10 pm**. What time does it start? Use morning, afternoon, noon or midnight with your answer.

6 The train to the seaside leaves the station at **twenty to eight** in the morning. It arrives at the seaside at **9:30 am**. How long does the journey take?

Calculate the time taken by particular events

1 A film lasted for an **hour**. For how many **minutes** did the film last?

2 Eliza went running at **10:20**. She returned at **10:45**. How long did Eliza run for?

3 Kasim went to the mosque at **4:30 pm**. He left at **5:20 pm**. How long did he stay at the mosque?

4 Blake went to bed when his clock read **15 minutes past 8**. He read until **8:40**. For how long did Blake read?

5 Lottie fell asleep at **9:15 pm**. The twittering birds woke her up at **4:15 am**. How long did Lottie sleep for?

6 Marcus played cricket from **1:30 pm** until **2:15 pm**. Hasim played for **half an hour**. How much longer did Marcus play cricket than Hasim?

Name ....

Calculate the time taken by particular events

1 Emile started his Maths lesson at **10:00 am**. It lasted for **50 minutes**. What time did it finish?

2 A bus takes **half an hour** to reach its destination. If it departs at **half past 8** in the morning, what time does it arrive?

3 Farzana started watching a film at **7:30 pm**. The film lasted for an **hour and a quarter**. What time did the film finish?

4 Mina takes **25 minutes** to eat her packed lunch. If she started eating at **12:15 pm**, what time would she finish?

5 Pippa's family set off for Funland Theme Park at **10:50 am**. The journey took **1 hour and 25 minutes**. What time did they arrive at the theme park?

6 Mr Young set off in his car at **3:10 pm**. He drove for **25 minutes** to pick up his daughter, Martha. He then drove for **35 minutes** to the park. What time did he arrive at the park?

Compare the duration of events

1 Maggie's favourite TV program lasted for **35 minutes**. Bart's lasted **half an hour**. Whose was shorter? By how much?

2 Clara and Maryam were running in a race. Clara finished the race in **12 minutes**. Maryam took a **quarter of an hour** to finish. Who finished the race **first**?

3 Katrina and Jenson started their homework at **4.15 pm**. Katrina finished in **45 minutes**. Jenson finished at **4:55 pm**. Who finished their homework **first**?

4 The train to the city takes **1 hour and 12 minutes**. The train to the countryside takes **88 minutes**. Which journey is longer?

5 In Class 3, on a Tuesday, they have Maths from **9:10 am** until break at **10:00 am**. After break, they have English from **11:00 am** until **11:55 am**. Which lesson is longer: English or Maths?

6 Declan completed the running section of the triathalon from **3 pm** until **4:30 pm**. He completed the swimming section from **4:30 pm** until **5:15 pm**. Which took him longer: running or swimming?

GEOMETRY

Properties of shapes

Describe and classify 2D and 3D shapes

1 Shaola draws a **quadrilateral**. How many sides does his shape have?

2 Georgie says a **pentagon** has **6** sides. Is she correct? Explain your answer.

3 How many sides do **two hexagons** have altogether?

4 Austin's homework is to draw **2** different types of **triangles**. Describe the **triangles** that Austin could draw using words or drawings or both.

5 What is the sum of the number of sides on a **hexagon** added to the number of sides on an **octagon**?

6 Katrina says that her cereal box is a **cuboid**. Name **two** other everyday objects that are **cuboids**.

Describe and classify 2D and 3D shapes

1 To draw a **cuboid**, would you need to use straight or curved lines?

2 What is the name of a **3D** shape which best describes a football?

3 What answer would you get if you added the number of sides on a **quadrilateral** to the number of sides on an **octagon**?

4 Draw a **2D** shape that has at least **one** line of symmetry.

5 Joshua names **two 2D** shapes that have **four** right angles each. What might they be?

6 Can you name **two 3D** shapes that have **eight** vertices?

Name ....

Describe and classify 2D and 3D shapes

1 Seth says a **heptagon** has **6** sides. Is he correct? Explain your answer.

2 A **triangular prism** has **5** faces. **3** of the faces are the same shape. What shape is this?

3 I am a **2D** shape. I have no straight sides. What shape am I?

4 If you added together the number of sides on a **triangle**, a **quadrilateral** and a **pentagon**, how many sides would there be altogether?

5 A **sphere** is a solid shape. A ball is a **sphere**. Can you explain why a **sphere** is a good shape for a ball?

6 A **cube** is a solid shape. A dice is a **cube**. Can you explain why a **cube** is a good shape for a dice?

Recognise angles as a property of shape and connect right angles and amount of turn

1 Brody writes the name of a shape that always has **four** right angles. What shape might Brody write?

2 Arif's class are making a shape dictionary. Complete Arif's description of a right-angled triangle.

"It has **3** sides and **three** angles.

One of the angles is a _____ _____."

3 The minute hand of a clock was pointing at **12**. Robbie moved it to point at **3**. What angle had the clock turned through?

4 Bogdan is facing the door. He makes a **half turn** to face the window. How many right angles has he turned through?

5 The minute hand of a clock turns from the number **3** to the number **5**. Tia said that it had turned more than a right angle. Is she correct? Explain your answer.

6 Summer did **5 full turns** very quickly in her ballet class. How many right angles did she turn through altogether?

Name ....

Identify horizontal and vertical lines and pairs of perpendicular and parallel lines

1 To draw a **rectangle**, would you use straight or curved lines?

2 Jafar draws **2** lines. The lines are the same distance apart all the way along their length. What kind of lines has he drawn?

3 Mr Little draws this line on the blackboard.

Has he drawn a **horizontal** or a **vertical** line? Explain your answer.

4 How many pairs of **parallel** lines does a **rectangle** have?

5 Why would it not be possible for a train to travel along tracks that were not **parallel**?

6 Explain the difference between **perpendicular** lines and **parallel** lines.

Name ....

STATISTICS

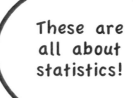

These are all about statistics!

Interpret data and solve problems from a tally chart

Tally chart to show the number of children in the playground at different times

Time	Tally
10 am	卌 |||
11 am	卌	
12 noon	|||
1 pm	卌 ||||
2 pm	卌 卌 |||

1 When are there the most children in the playground?

2 How many more children were in the playground at **11 am** than at **12 noon**?

3 Why do you think there were the least number of children in the playground at **12 noon**?

4 How many children were in the playground in total during the afternoon (including those in at **12 noon**)?

5 Chloe said, "There were **twice** as many children in the playground at **2 pm** as there were at **11 am**." Is she correct? Explain your answer.

Interpret data and solve problems from a tally chart

Tally chart to show the number of animals seen in the park on Tuesday afternoon

Animal		Tally
birds		卌 |||
rabbits		|||
dogs		卌	
cats		
worms		卌 卌 |||

1 How many birds were there in the park?

2 How many cats were there in the park?

3 How many more birds were there than rabbits?

4 How many more worms were there than dogs?

5 Why do you think that there were no cats in the park during the afternoon?

6 How many creatures were counted in total in the park?

Name ....

Interpret data and solve problems from a tally chart

Tally chart to show the number of animals on the farm

Animal		Tally
horses		卌 ||
cows		|||
sheep		卌
pigs		卌 ||||

1 How many cows are on the farm?

2 How many pigs are on the farm?

3 How many more horses are there than cows?

4 Kate says, "There are more pigs than there are cows and sheep put together." Is this true? Explain how you know.

5 How many animals are there in total?

Interpret data and solve problems from a bar chart

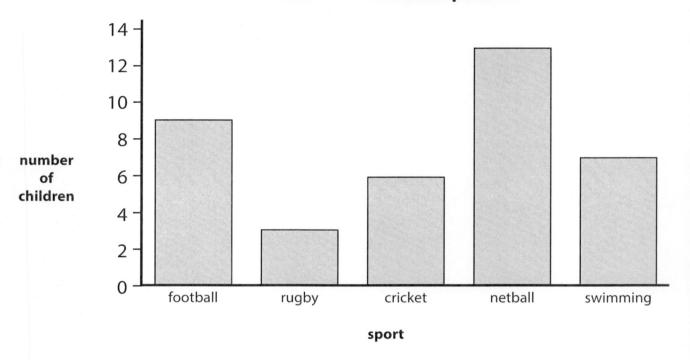

Bar chart to show the favourite sports of Year 3

1. What is the most popular sport in Year 3?

2. How many people said they like cricket?

3. How many people said they like swimming?

4. How many people said they like either football or cricket?

5. How many more people like netball than rugby?

6. If **3** people changed their mind and said they liked cricket and not football, how many more people would like cricket than football?

Interpret data and solve problems from a bar chart

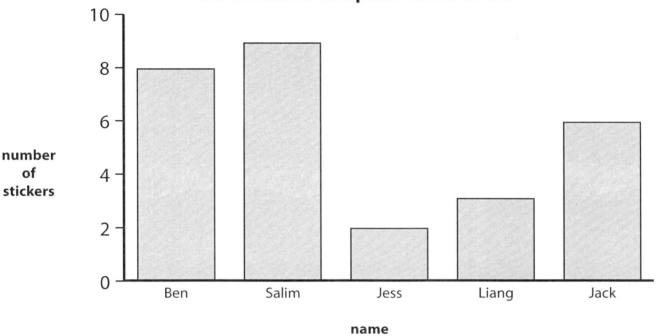

Bar chart to show how many stickers are needed to complete sticker books

1 Who has collected the most stickers so far?

2 How many stickers have Jess and Liang collected altogether?

3 How many more stickers has Salim collected than Jack?

4 How many stickers less than Ben has Liang collected?

5 How many stickers have they collected altogther?

6 If **10** stickers are needed to complete each person's sticker book, how many more stickers do the children need to collect altogether?

Interpret data and solve problems from a bar chart

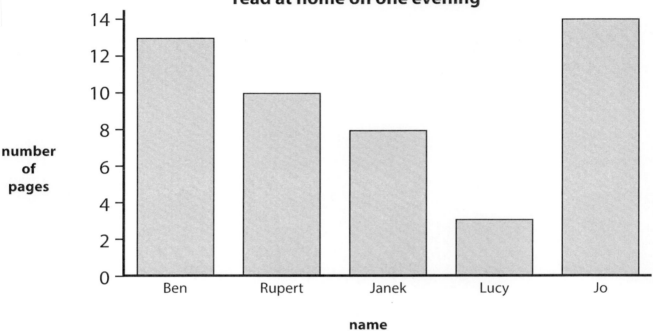

Bar chart to show how many pages of their book children read at home on one evening

1 Who read the most pages?

2 How many pages did Janek read?

3 How many pages did Ben read?

4 How many more pages did Jo read than Rupert?

5 Why do you think Lucy only read **3** pages?

6 How many pages did all **five** children read between them?

106

Name ....

Interpret data and solve problems from a pictogram

Pictogram to show how Year 3 travel to school

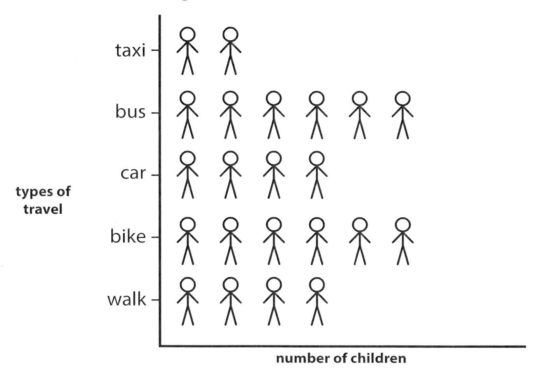

types of
travel

number of children

1. How many children go to school by bus?

2. How many children go to school by taxi?

3. How many children go to school either by bike or by walking?

4. How many more children walk than go in the car?

5. How many more children go by bus than by taxi?

6. Do you think that most children live very near to the school? Explain your answer.

107   Name ....

Interpret data and solve problems from a pictogram

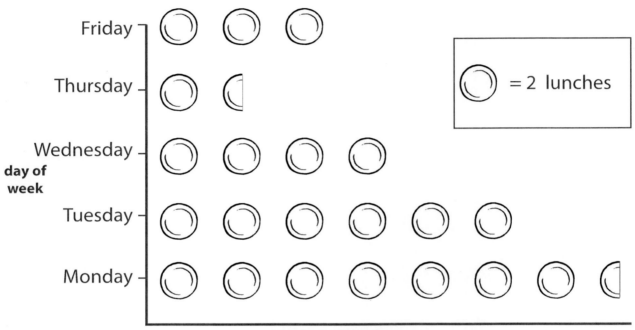

Pictogram to show the number of hot lunches eaten by Class 3

○ = 2 lunches

day of
week

number of lunches

1 How many hot lunches were eaten on Tuesday?

2 What was the most popular day for eating hot lunches?

3 How many hot lunches were eaten on Thursday?

4 How many more hot lunches were eaten on Tuesday than on Wednesday?

5 How many more hot lunches were eaten on Monday than on Thursday?

6 How many hot lunches were eaten in total during the week?

Interpret data and solve problems from a pictogram

Pictogram to show colour of bikes sold in a week

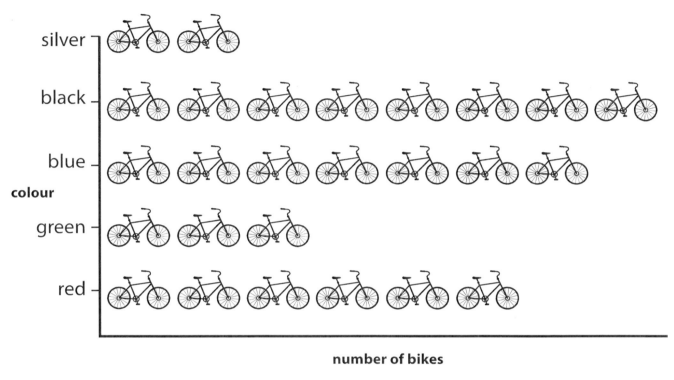

colour

number of bikes

1 What is the most popular colour of bikes sold this week?

2 How many red bikes are sold?

3 How many silver and blue bikes are sold?

4 How many more blue bikes are sold than green bikes?

5 Ola says, "Black and red together sold **twice** as many as blue." Is she correct? Explain your answer.

6 Using the pictogram, make up a question that you could ask a friend about the bikes.

   Name ....

Interpret data and solve problems from a table

Day	Number of cars in the car park
Monday	11
Tuesday	13
Wednesday	17
Thursday	6
Friday	12

1 How many cars were in the car park on Friday?

2 On which day were there the most cars in the car park?

3 How many cars were there on the **first three** days?

4 How many more cars were there on Wednesday than on Thursday?

5 Which day has **twice** as many cars as the day before?

6 Using the frequency table, write a question that you could ask about cars in the car park.

Name ....

Interpret data and solve problems from a table

Table to show the number of children in the swimming pool

	10 am	11 am	12 noon	1 pm	2 pm
Saturday	8	7	6	7	12
Sunday	7	8	5	6	11

1 How many children were in the pool on **Saturday** at **10 am**?

2 How many more people were in the pool at **2 pm** on **Sunday** than **12 noon** on **Saturday**?

3 Why do you think there were the least number of children in the pool at **12 noon**?

4 How many children were in the pool on **Sunday** afternoon (including **12 noon**)?

5 Miguel, the lifeguard, said, "There were **half** as many children in the pool at **1 pm** on **Sunday** than there were at **2 pm** on **Saturday**." Is he correct? Explain your answer.

6 He also said, "There were more people in the pool at each time on **Saturday** than on **Sunday**." Is he correct? Explain your answer.

Interpret data and solve problems from a table

Name of child	Number of team points gained in a week
Chloe	16
Paige	15
Asmat	19
Rio	10
Mo	8

1 Who got the most team points during the week?

2 Who got **twice** as many team points as Mo?

3 How many team points did Rio get?

4 How many more team points did Paige get than Mo?

5 How many more team points did Asmat get than Mo and Rio put together?

6 How many team points did all **five** children get between them?

Name ....

Year 3: NUMBER – Number and place value

Page 1: 1) 8 2) 12 3) 16 4) 32 5) 50, 100 6) 300

Page 2: 1) 12 2) 8 3) 300 4) 50, 100, 150 5) 400 6) 12, 20, 24

Page 3: 1) 4 2) 4 3) 12 4) 10 5) 866 6) 5

Page 4: 1) 9 2) 12, 14, 16 3) 30 4) 20, 24 5) 190 6) 232, 332, 432, 532

Page 5: 1) 100 2) 77 3) 74 4) 15 5) 324 6) 17

Page 6: 1) 48 2) 247 3) 76 4) 82 5) 434 6) £156

Page 7: 1) 2 2) 3 3) 5 4) 4 5) 60 6) 329

Page 8: 1) 400 + 80 + 2 2) 287 3) 746 4) no; appropriate explanation 5) no; appropriate explanation

Page 9: 1) 428; appropriate explanation 2) 320, 310, 305, 300 3) 536 4) 224; appropriate explanation 5) 349 6) 345, 354, 435, 534, 543

Page 10: 1) 820, 840, 865, 882 2) 895 3) 690, 658, 641, 630 4) 490 5) 981, 918, 899, 891, 819

Page 11: 1) 30 2) Holly (7 m) 3) 10 m 4) girls (36) 5) 50 6) Benny (135 cm)

Page 12: 1) 100 ml 2) yes; appropriate explanation 3) 800; appropriate explanation 4) 5 5) 700 ml

Page 13: 1) seventy two 2) 230 3) 343 4) 862 5) seven hundred and eighty seven 6) eight hundred and fifty three

Page 14: 1) eight 2) 15 3) two hundred and fifty two 4) 464 5) three hundred and forty eight 6) eight hundred and seventy six

Page 15: 1) 90p 2) £2.67 3) £100 4) £398 5) 5 in £650 6) £126

Page 16: 1) 90 ml 2) Wednesday (8 lengths) 3) Billy (132 cm) 4) 10 kg 5) on the way; appropriate explanation

Page 17: 1) 20 2) 30 3) 46 4) 204 5) eldest - Liam, youngest - Jasmin 6) appropriate explanation

Page 18: 1) 112 2) two hundred and fifty six 3) 900 g 4) 643 5) 16

Page 19: 1) 50 2) 452 3) 9 4) 4 5) appropriate examples 6) 32

Page 20: 1) 24 2) one hundred and forty three 3) 126 4) 260 g 5) appropriate explanation 6) 80

Year 3: NUMBER - Addition and subtraction

Page 21: 1) 119 2) 259 3) 112 4) 134 5) 146 6) 139

Page 22: 1) 115 2) 120 3) 166 4) 138 5) 232 miles 6) 126

Page 23: 1) 111 2) 225 3) 132 4) 393 5) £86

Page 24: 1) 142 2) 144 3) 210 4) 47 5) 243

Page 25: 1) 40 2) 92 3) 88 4) 122 5) 34 6) 152

Page 26: 1) 12 2) 110 3) 150 cm 4) 113 5) 46 cm 6) 213

Page 27: 1) 208 2) 325 3) 337 4) 638 5) 447 6) 878

Page 28: 1) 150 2) 80 3) 157 4) 80 5) 317

Page 29: 1) 345 2) 128 3) 475 g 4) 362 5) 356

Page 30: 1) 88, 130 2) 142 3) 381 4) 510 5) 330

Page 31: 1) £34 2) 64 3) 48 4) 348 5) 339

Page 32: 1) 213 2) 231 3) 440 4) 157 5) 380 cm

Page 33: 1) yes; appropriate explanation 2) 50 + 50 3) yes ; appropriate explanation 4) 100
          5) 100 6) 450

Page 34: 1) 10 - 2 = 8 or 10 - 8 = 2 2) no; appropriate explanation 3) 7 + 8 = 15 4) 16 - 7 = 9 or
          16 - 9 = 7 5) 112 - 80 = 32 or 112 - 32 = 80 6) 19 + 78 = 97 or 78 + 19 = 97

Page 35: 1) appropriate explanation 2) 36 3) 16 4) 698 5) 20 - 8 = 12, 21 - 8 = 13,
          appropriate calculation

Page 36: 1) £1.75 2) £2.48 3) £3.10 4) £2.79 5) 35p 6) no; appropriate explanation

Page 37: 1) 42p 2) £2.25 3) £5.25 4) £72 5) £63 6) £60

Page 38: 1) 90 2) 37p 3) 49 4) 36 5) 116 6) 215

Page 39: 1) 45 2) 41p 3) 158 4) 30 5) 86

Page 40: 1) 87 2) £4.50 3) 196 4) 20 5) 616 6) 356

Year 3: NUMBER - Multiplication and division

Page 41: 1) £12 2) 15 3) 12 4) 21 miles 5) 30 6) 240p

Page 42: 1) 8 2) 12 3) 16 4) 40 5) 28 6) 48

Page 43: 1) 16 2) 24 3) 48 4) 56 5) 64 6) 96

Page 44: 1) 16 2) 12 3) 24 4) 64 5) 44 6) 36

Page 45: 1) 8 2) 32 3) 30 4) 24 5) 96 6) 49

Page 46: 1) 3 2) 6 3) 5 4) 8 5) 9 6) 12

Page 47: 1) 2 2) 3 3) 4 4) 6 5) 8 6) 12, 13

Page 48: 1) 2 2) 4 3) 7 4) 8 5) 8 6) 11, 96

Page 49: 1) 3 2) 2 3) 6 4) 3 5) 12 6) 9

Page 50: 1) 3 2) 4 3) £7 4) 12 5) 9 6) 12

Page 51: 1) 12 2) 5 3) 8 4) 9 5) £8 6) 13

Page 52: 1) 24 2) £40 3) 48 4) 7 5) £36 6) 6

Page 53: 1) appropriate explanation 2) appropriate explanation 3) 16 4) 64
          5) 48; appropriate explanation

Page 54: 1) 48 2) 80 m 3) 120p 4) 69 5) 132 6) 212

Page 55: 1) 96 2) 76 3) 150 4) £104 5) 135 6) 168

Page 56: 1) 9 2) 8 3) 20p 4) 15 5) 40 6) £13

Page 57: 1) 14 2) 8 3) 15 4) 32 5) 12 6) 21

Page 58: 1) 88 2) 72 3) 260 4) 136 5) 128p 6) 24 x 8

Page 59: 1) 21 2) 14 3) 24 4) 12 5) 12, 3

Page 60: 1) £64 2) 13 3) 11, 6 4) 78 5) 368 6) 32, 1

Page 61: 1) 400 cm 2) 56 3) 140 cm 4) 90 g 5) 104

Year 3: NUMBER - Fractions

Page 62: 1) $\frac{9}{10}$ 2) $\frac{8}{10}$ 3) $\frac{3}{10}$ 4) $\frac{4}{10}$ 5) $\frac{3}{10}$ 6) $\frac{5}{10}$

Page 63: 1) 16 2) 9 3) 5 4) 5 5) 3 6) £54

Page 64: 1) 10 2) 30; appropriate explanation 3) 9 4) 18 5) 45

Page 65: 1) yes; appropriate explanation 2) no; appropriate explanation 3) appropriate explanation 4) yes 5) no; appropriate explanation

Page 66: 1) 5 2) 5 3) 3 4) 14 5) 19

Page 67: 1) $\frac{2}{3}$ 2) $\frac{3}{4}$ 3) $\frac{4}{5}$ 4) $\frac{5}{7}$ 5) $\frac{7}{8}$

Page 68: 1) $\frac{1}{3}$ 2) $\frac{2}{5}$ 3) $\frac{2}{4}$ 4) $\frac{3}{6}$ 5) $\frac{1}{8}$

Page 69: 1) $\frac{3}{4}$ 2) $\frac{2}{3}$ 3) $\frac{5}{6}$ 4) $\frac{1}{5}$ 5) $\frac{1}{5}$ 6) $\frac{6}{8}$

Page 70: 1) $\frac{3}{4}$ 2) Bubbles ($\frac{2}{3}$) 3) Jake; appropriate explanation 4) Caitlin had the most, James had the least 5) $\frac{1}{8}$, $\frac{3}{8}$, $\frac{4}{8}$, $\frac{7}{8}$

Page 71: 1) 100 ml 2) £5 3) 5 4) 10 5) 2 kg 6) 1/2 of £24

Page 72: 1) $\frac{7}{8}$ 2) $\frac{2}{6}$ 3) They have the same amount; appropriate explanation 4) 5 5) no; appropriate explanation 6) £28

Page 73: 1) 5 2) appropriate shading 3) 0.5 4) $\frac{3}{8}$ 5) appropriate explanation 6) £36

Year 3: MEASUREMENT

Page 74: 1) Paul's (32 cm) 2) Tom's (45.5 cm) 3) Harriet (8.6 cm) 4) kitchen 5) Ollie 6) May - 1.2 m, July - 0.9 m

Page 75: 1) Kim's (80g) 2) red (180 g) 3) glass-top (86.5 kg) 4) Dad (64.4 kg) 5) Tommy (202 kg) 6) Mrs Whitford's is the heaviest, Mrs Jackson's is the lightest

Page 76: 1) Rachel 2) Lisa 3) green jug 4) Fish Tank B 5) Frankie 6) Adam's has the most, Zara's has the least

Page 77: 1) Brown 2) Mum 3) Fence B 4) Hoxley 5) walking past the park; 9 m 6) Josh (1356 ml), Aden (110 cm)

Page 78: 1) 900 cm 2) 141 cm 3) 27 cm 4) 1 m 19 cm 5) 47 m 6) 22 cm

Page 79: 1) 100 g 2) 35 g 3) 75 g 4) 215 g 5) 15 kg 6) 2 loaves, 300 g left

Page 80: 1) 30 ml 2) 230 ml 3) 100 ml 4) 4.5 l 5) 50 l 6) 23 l

Page 81: 1) 84 cm 2) 300 ml 3) 1.62 m 4) 102 km 5) 120 cm 6) 9.5 km

Page 82: 1) 50 m 2) 111 cm 3) 625 ml 4) 17 cm 5) 135 cm 6) 1750 g

Page 83: 1) £1.90 2) £4.35 3) 60p 4) 35p 5) £1.80 6) key ring, ball, pen and pencil set

Page 84: 1) 60p 2) 35p 3) £8 4) £2 5) £1.10 6) no; appropriate explanation

Page 85: 1) £1.00 2) £1.90 3) £2.50 4) 55p 5) 90p 6) £2.30 7) £4.00

Page 86: 1) 255p 2) £3.70 3) 30p 4) £1.90 5) Big Wheel and Twister; Dodgems, Twister and Ghost Train; Space Stroller and Dodgems

Page 87: 1) 120 seconds 2) Paul, 10 seconds 3) yes; appropriate explanation 4) 120 minutes
5) Imran 6) 240 minutes

Page 88: 1) afternoon 2) appropriate explanation 3) no; appropriate explanation
4) no; appropriate explanation 5) no; appropriate explanation 6) 12 midnight

Page 89: 1) 60 seconds 2) 15 seconds 3) 120 seconds 4) 1 ½ minutes 5) 300 seconds
6) 240 seconds

Page 90: 1) 31 days 2) July 3) February, November, May 4) 61 days 5) 60 days 6) 122 days

Page 91: 1) 365 days 2) 4 years 3) 366 days 4) 304 days 5) 93 days 6) 323 days

Page 92: 1) 120 seconds 2) 2 pm 3) 6 minutes 4) 4:10pm 5) 12 noon 6) 1 hour 50 minutes

Page 93: 1) 60 minutes 2) 25 minutes 3) 50 minutes 4) 25 minutes 5) 7 hours 6) 15 minutes

Page 94: 1) 10:50 am 2) 9 am 3) 8:45 pm 4) 12:40 pm 5) 12:15 pm 6) 4:10 pm

Page 95: 1) Bart's, 5 minutes 2) Clara 3) Jenson 4) train to countryside 5) English 6) running

Year 3: GEOMETRY - Properties of shapes

Page 96: 1) 4 2) no; appropriate explanation 3) 12 4) appropriate descriptions 5) 14
6) appropriate objects named

Page 97: 1) straight 2) sphere 3) 12 4) appropriate drawing 5) square, rectangle 6) cube, cuboid

Page 98: 1) no; appropriate explanation 2) rectangle 3) circle 4) 12 5) appropriate explanation
6) appropriate explanation

Page 99: 1) square, rectangle 2) right angle 3) 90° 4) 2 5) no; appropriate explanation 6) 20

Page 100: 1) straight 2) parallel 3) vertical; appropriate explanation 4) 2
5) appropriate explanation 6) appropriate explanation

Year 3: STATISTICS

Page 101: 1) 2pm 2) 3 3) lunch 4) 25 5) no; appropriate explanation

Page 102: 1) 8 2) 0 3) 5 4) 7 5) appropriate explanation 6) 30

Page 103: 1) 3 2) 9 3) 4 4) yes; appropriate explanation 5) 24

Page 104: 1) netball 2) 6 3) 7 4) 15 5) 10 6) 3

Page 105: 1) Salim 2) 5 3) 3 4) 5 5) 28 6) 22

Page 106: 1) Jo 2) 8 3) 13 4) 4 5) appropriate explanation 6) 48

Page 107: 1) 6 2) 2 3) 10 4) 0 5) 4 6) appropriate explanation

Page 108: 1) 12 2) Monday 3) 3 4) 5 5) 12 6) 44

Page 109: 1) black 2) 6 3) 9 4) 4 5) yes; appropriate explanation 6) appropriate question

Page 110: 1) 12 2) Wednesday 3) 41 4) 11 5) Friday 6) appropriate question

Page 111: 1) 8 2) 5 3) appropriate explanation 4) 22 5) yes; appropriate explanation 6) no;
appropriate explanation

Page 112: 1) Asmat 2) Chloe 3) 10 4) 7 5) 1 6) 68